THE BEERMAKER'S

RECORD BOOK

A Record Book of Beers Made by

_____

THE BEERMAKER'S

RECORD BOOK

RAINCOAST BOOKS
Vancouver

Copyright © 1997 by Raincoast Book Distribution Ltd.

All rights reserved. No part of this publication may be reproduced or transmitted in any form or by any means, electronic or mechanical, including photocopying, recording, or by any information storage and retrieval system, now known or to be invented, without permission in writing from the publisher.

First published in 1997 by

Raincoast Books
8680 Cambie Street
Vancouver, B.C.
V6P 6M9
(604) 323-7100

1 2 3 4 5 6 7 8 9 10

CANADIAN CATALOGUING IN PUBLICATION DATA

Main entry under title:

The beermaker's record book

ISBN 1-55192-115-4

1. Brewing. 2. Beer. 3. Blank-books.
TP570.B43 1997   641.8'73   C97-910454-8

Printed and bound in Canada

CONTENTS

Introduction *9*

Beermaking and Tasting Notes *11*

Additional Comments and Labels *80*

Addresses and Contact Numbers *88*

Beer-Tasting Terms *93*

AFRIKAANS	BIER
CANTONESE	BE JÁU
CATALAN	CERVESA
CHINESE	PI JIU
CREOLE	BYÈ
CZECH	PIVO
DANSK	ØL
DUTCH	BIER
FINNISH	OLUT
FRENCH	BIÈRE
GERMAN	BIER
HAUSA	GIYÀ
HAWAIIAN	BIA NUI
HUNGARIAN	SÖR
ICELANDIC	BJÓR
IRISH	BEIOR
ITALIAN	BIRRA
JAPANESE	BIIRU
KOREAN	MAEK-JU
LITHUANIAN	ALUS'
NORSK	ØL
NORWEGIAN	ØL'
POLISH	PIWO
PORTUGESE	CERVEJA
ROMANIAN	BERE
RUSSIAN	PEEVA
SPANISH	CERVEZA
SWEDISH	ÖL
THAI	BEE-A
TURKISH	BIRA
VIETNAMESE	RUOU BIA
YIDDISH	BIR
ZULU	UTSHWALA

INTRODUCTION

On the divine noble gift, the philosophical, highly dear and wondrous art, to brew beer.
   – Erfurt, 1583

Welcome to the world of beermaking. Whether you are new to brewing your own beers or an old hand at it, *The Beermaker's Record Book* is intended to be a companion to your beermaking activities. A convenient place to document all of your beermaking successes (and, possibly, some of those yields that just leave you flat), this record book will help you to keep track of the many details involved in preparing each batch of beer, including the amount of essential ingredients that you place in each recipe as well as the vital statistics of your final brew.

Making beer can be an elaborate undertaking, but when it comes right down to it, your ultimate goal is simple: to produce beer that both you and the people around you will enjoy drinking. While *The Beermaker's Record Book* is neither a technical guide nor a how-to book, it *is* intended to heighten your enjoyment of the beermaking process by providing a place for you to rate your final product as well as comment on the tastes, flavors, and many other distinguishing features of your beer creations. Beermaking is a labor of love and learning, and because each beer and the conditions under which it is made can vary, this book also serves as a handy reference guide for future batches. Additional space has been provided for you to record your observations on the various beers that you have made, as well as your comments on, for example, what food might complement them or what type of brew to attempt next time.

With space provided to paste in your favorite labels; a section for the addresses and contact numbers of beer stores, supply shops, fellow beermakers, brew clubs, or friends who just love to imbibe; and a glossary of specialized beer-tasting terms, this book serves as an ideal personal resource for your beermaking endeavors.

Enjoy!

BEERMAKING AND TASTING NOTES

A quart of ale is a dish for a king.
– William Shakespeare, *The Winter's Tale*

THE BEERMAKER'S RECORD BOOK

Who & Where

BEERMAKING SITE	CO-BEERMAKERS

The Details

RECIPE No.	% ALCOHOL
COMMERCIAL NAME	BOTTLE SIZE
BREWCASTLE NAME	$ per DOZ.
TYPE of BREW	$ per BATCH
DESCRIPTION	DATE MADE
	DATE BOTTLED
	No. of BOTTLES

Recipe Sheet

MALT (vol. per)	
FERMENTABLES	
GRAIN (wt. per)	
HOPS (wt. per)	
YEAST (wt. or amt.)	
ADDITIONAL NOTES	

Vital Stats

ORIGINAL SPECIFIC GRAVITY (og)	ALCOHOL by VOLUME
FINAL SPECIFIC GRAVITY (fg)	COLOR (srms)
APPARENT DEGREE of ACTUAL FERMENTATION	BITTERNESS (ibus)

RECORDS

First Tasting

DATE	WEEKS after BOTTLING
TASTERS PRESENT	
COMMENTS	

Second Tasting

DATE	WEEKS after BOTTLING
TASTERS PRESENT	
COMMENTS	

Tasting Notes

AROMA	OVERALL IMPRESSION
COLOR/APPEARANCE	
FLAVOR	
MOUTHFEEL/BODY	

OVERALL RATING

☐ FLOP   ☐ DRINKABLE   ☐ MOST ENJOYABLE   ☐ EXCEPTIONAL

Beer tasting usually involves evaluating the following five features in the order given: (1) aroma; (2) color and appearance; (3) flavor; (4) mouthfeel and body; (5) overall impression and aftertaste. (See Glossary for definitions.)

THE BEERMAKER'S RECORD BOOK

Who & Where

BEERMAKING SITE	CO-BEERMAKERS

The Details

RECIPE No.	% ALCOHOL
COMMERCIAL NAME	BOTTLE SIZE
BREWCASTLE NAME	$ per DOZ.
TYPE of BREW	$ per BATCH
DESCRIPTION	DATE MADE
	DATE BOTTLED
	No. of BOTTLES

Recipe Sheet

MALT (VOL. per)	
FERMENTABLES	
GRAIN (WT. per)	
HOPS (WT. per)		
YEAST (WT. or AMT.)	
ADDITIONAL NOTES	

Vital Stats

ORIGINAL SPECIFIC GRAVITY (OG)	ALCOHOL by VOLUME
FINAL SPECIFIC GRAVITY (FG)	COLOR (SRMS)
APPARENT DEGREE of ACTUAL FERMENTATION	BITTERNESS (IBUS)

RECORDS

DATE	WEEKS after BOTTLING
TASTERS PRESENT	
COMMENTS	

First Tasting

DATE	WEEKS after BOTTLING
TASTERS PRESENT	
COMMENTS	

Second Tasting

AROMA	OVERALL IMPRESSION
COLOR/APPEARANCE	
FLAVOR	
MOUTHFEEL/BODY	

Tasting Notes

OVERALL RATING

☐ FLOP   ☐ DRINKABLE   ☐ MOST ENJOYABLE   ☐ EXCEPTIONAL

Beer tasting usually involves evaluating the following five features in the order given: (1) aroma; (2) color and appearance; (3) flavor; (4) mouthfeel and body; (5) overall impression and aftertaste. (See Glossary for definitions.)

THE BEERMAKER'S RECORD BOOK

Who & Where

BEERMAKING SITE	CO-BEERMAKERS

The Details

RECIPE No.	% ALCOHOL
COMMERCIAL NAME	BOTTLE SIZE
BREWCASTLE NAME	$ per DOZ.
TYPE of BREW	$ per BATCH
DESCRIPTION	DATE MADE
	DATE BOTTLED
	No. of BOTTLES

Recipe Sheet

MALT (VOL. per)	
FERMENTABLES	
GRAIN (WT. per)	
HOPS (WT. per)		
YEAST (WT. or AMT.)	
ADDITIONAL NOTES	

Vital Stats

ORIGINAL SPECIFIC GRAVITY (OG)	ALCOHOL by VOLUME
FINAL SPECIFIC GRAVITY (FG)	COLOR (SRMS)
APPARENT DEGREE of ACTUAL FERMENTATION	BITTERNESS (IBUS)

RECORDS

DATE	WEEKS after BOTTLING
TASTERS PRESENT	
COMMENTS	

First Tasting

DATE	WEEKS after BOTTLING
TASTERS PRESENT	
COMMENTS	

Second Tasting

AROMA	OVERALL IMPRESSION
COLOR/APPEARANCE	
FLAVOR	
MOUTHFEEL/BODY	

Tasting Notes

OVERALL RATING

☐ FLOP ☐ DRINKABLE ☐ MOST ENJOYABLE ☐ EXCEPTIONAL

Beer tasting usually involves evaluating the following five features in the order given: (1) aroma; (2) color and appearance; (3) flavor; (4) mouthfeel and body; (5) overall impression and aftertaste. (See Glossary for definitions.)

THE BEERMAKER'S RECORD BOOK

Who & Where

BEERMAKING SITE	CO-BEERMAKERS

The Details

RECIPE No.	% ALCOHOL
COMMERCIAL NAME	BOTTLE SIZE
BREWCASTLE NAME	$ per DOZ.
TYPE of BREW	$ per BATCH
DESCRIPTION	DATE MADE
	DATE BOTTLED
	No. of BOTTLES

Recipe Sheet

MALT (VOL. per)	
FERMENTABLES	
GRAIN (WT. per)	
HOPS (WT. per)		
YEAST (WT. or AMT.)	
ADDITIONAL NOTES	

Vital Stats

ORIGINAL SPECIFIC GRAVITY (OG)	ALCOHOL by VOLUME
FINAL SPECIFIC GRAVITY (FG)	COLOR (SRMS)
APPARENT DEGREE of ACTUAL FERMENTATION	BITTERNESS (IBUS)

RECORDS

First Tasting

DATE		WEEKS after BOTTLING
TASTERS PRESENT		
COMMENTS		

Second Tasting

DATE		WEEKS after BOTTLING
TASTERS PRESENT		
COMMENTS		

Tasting Notes

	OVERALL IMPRESSION
AROMA	
COLOR/APPEARANCE	
FLAVOR	
MOUTHFEEL/BODY	

OVERALL RATING

☐ FLOP   ☐ DRINKABLE   ☐ MOST ENJOYABLE   ☐ EXCEPTIONAL

Beer tasting usually involves evaluating the following five features in the order given: (1) aroma; (2) color and appearance; (3) flavor; (4) mouthfeel and body; (5) overall impression and aftertaste. (See Glossary for definitions.)

THE BEERMAKER'S RECORD BOOK

Who & Where

BEERMAKING SITE	CO-BEERMAKERS

The Details

RECIPE No.	% ALCOHOL
COMMERCIAL NAME	BOTTLE SIZE
BREWCASTLE NAME	$ per DOZ.
TYPE of BREW	$ per BATCH
DESCRIPTION	DATE MADE
	DATE BOTTLED
	No. of BOTTLES

Recipe Sheet

MALT (vol. per)		
FERMENTABLES		
GRAIN (wt. per)		
HOPS (wt. per)		
YEAST (wt. or amt.)		
ADDITIONAL NOTES		

Vital Stats

ORIGINAL SPECIFIC GRAVITY (og)	ALCOHOL by VOLUME
FINAL SPECIFIC GRAVITY (fg)	COLOR (srms)
APPARENT DEGREE of ACTUAL FERMENTATION	BITTERNESS (ibus)

RECORDS

DATE		WEEKS after BOTTLING
TASTERS PRESENT		
COMMENTS		

First Tasting

DATE		WEEKS after BOTTLING
TASTERS PRESENT		
COMMENTS		

Second Tasting

AROMA	OVERALL IMPRESSION
COLOR/APPEARANCE	
FLAVOR	
MOUTHFEEL/BODY	

Tasting Notes

OVERALL RATING

☐ FLOP   ☐ DRINKABLE   ☐ MOST ENJOYABLE   ☐ EXCEPTIONAL

Beer tasting usually involves evaluating the following five features in the order given: (1) aroma; (2) color and appearance; (3) flavor; (4) mouthfeel and body; (5) overall impression and aftertaste. (See Glossary for definitions.)

THE BEERMAKER'S RECORD BOOK

Who & Where

BEERMAKING SITE	CO-BEERMAKERS

The Details

RECIPE No.	% ALCOHOL
COMMERCIAL NAME	BOTTLE SIZE
BREWCASTLE NAME	$ per DOZ.
TYPE of BREW	$ per BATCH
DESCRIPTION	DATE MADE
	DATE BOTTLED
	No. of BOTTLES

Recipe Sheet

MALT (vol. per)	
FERMENTABLES	
GRAIN (wt. per)	
HOPS (wt. per)	
YEAST (wt. or amt.)	
ADDITIONAL NOTES	

Vital Stats

ORIGINAL SPECIFIC GRAVITY (og)	ALCOHOL by VOLUME
FINAL SPECIFIC GRAVITY (fg)	COLOR (srms)
APPARENT DEGREE of ACTUAL FERMENTATION	BITTERNESS (ibus)

RECORDS

DATE	WEEKS after BOTTLING
TASTERS PRESENT	
COMMENTS	

First Tasting

DATE	WEEKS after BOTTLING
TASTERS PRESENT	
COMMENTS	

Second Tasting

AROMA	OVERALL IMPRESSION
COLOR/APPEARANCE	
FLAVOR	
MOUTHFEEL/BODY	

Tasting Notes

OVERALL RATING

☐ FLOP ☐ DRINKABLE ☐ MOST ENJOYABLE ☐ EXCEPTIONAL

Beer tasting usually involves evaluating the following five features in the order given: (1) aroma; (2) color and appearance; (3) flavor; (4) mouthfeel and body; (5) overall impression and aftertaste. (See Glossary for definitions.)

THE BEERMAKER'S RECORD BOOK

Who & Where

BEERMAKING SITE	CO-BEERMAKERS

The Details

RECIPE No.	% ALCOHOL
COMMERCIAL NAME	BOTTLE SIZE
BREWCASTLE NAME	$ per DOZ.
TYPE of BREW	$ per BATCH
DESCRIPTION	DATE MADE
	DATE BOTTLED
	No. of BOTTLES

Recipe Sheet

MALT (VOL. per)			
FERMENTABLES			
GRAIN (WT. per)			
HOPS (WT. per)			
YEAST (WT. or AMT.)			
ADDITIONAL NOTES			

Vital Stats

ORIGINAL SPECIFIC GRAVITY (OG)	ALCOHOL by VOLUME
FINAL SPECIFIC GRAVITY (FG)	COLOR (SRMS)
APPARENT DEGREE of ACTUAL FERMENTATION	BITTERNESS (IBUS)

RECORDS

DATE	WEEKS after BOTTLING
TASTERS PRESENT	
COMMENTS	

First Tasting

DATE	WEEKS after BOTTLING
TASTERS PRESENT	
COMMENTS	

Second Tasting

AROMA	OVERALL IMPRESSION
COLOR/APPEARANCE	
FLAVOR	
MOUTHFEEL/BODY	

Tasting Notes

OVERALL RATING

☐ FLOP   ☐ DRINKABLE   ☐ MOST ENJOYABLE   ☐ EXCEPTIONAL

Beer tasting usually involves evaluating the following five features in the order given: (1) aroma; (2) color and appearance; (3) flavor; (4) mouthfeel and body; (5) overall impression and aftertaste. (See Glossary for definitions.)

THE BEERMAKER'S RECORD BOOK

Who & Where

BEERMAKING SITE	CO-BEERMAKERS

The Details

RECIPE No.	% ALCOHOL
COMMERCIAL NAME	BOTTLE SIZE
BREWCASTLE NAME	$ per DOZ.
TYPE of BREW	$ per BATCH
DESCRIPTION	DATE MADE
	DATE BOTTLED
	No. of BOTTLES

Recipe Sheet

MALT (VOL. per)	
FERMENTABLES	
GRAIN (WT. per)	
HOPS (WT. per)		
YEAST (WT. or AMT.)	
ADDITIONAL NOTES	

Vital Stats

ORIGINAL SPECIFIC GRAVITY (OG)	ALCOHOL by VOLUME
FINAL SPECIFIC GRAVITY (FG)	COLOR (SRMS)
APPARENT DEGREE of ACTUAL FERMENTATION	BITTERNESS (IBUS)

RECORDS

DATE	WEEKS after BOTTLING
TASTERS PRESENT	
COMMENTS	

First Tasting

DATE	WEEKS after BOTTLING
TASTERS PRESENT	
COMMENTS	

Second Tasting

	OVERALL IMPRESSION
AROMA	
COLOR/APPEARANCE	
FLAVOR	
MOUTHFEEL/BODY	

Tasting Notes

OVERALL RATING

☐ FLOP   ☐ DRINKABLE   ☐ MOST ENJOYABLE   ☐ EXCEPTIONAL

Beer tasting usually involves evaluating the following five features in the order given: (1) aroma; (2) color and appearance; (3) flavor; (4) mouthfeel and body; (5) overall impression and aftertaste. (See Glossary for definitions.)

THE BEERMAKER'S RECORD BOOK

Who & Where

BEERMAKING SITE	CO-BEERMAKERS

The Details

RECIPE No.	% ALCOHOL
COMMERCIAL NAME	BOTTLE SIZE
BREWCASTLE NAME	$ per DOZ.
TYPE of BREW	$ per BATCH
DESCRIPTION	DATE MADE
	DATE BOTTLED
	No. of BOTTLES

Recipe Sheet

MALT (vol. per)	
FERMENTABLES	
GRAIN (wt. per)	
HOPS (wt. per)		
YEAST (wt. or amt.)	
ADDITIONAL NOTES	

Vital Stats

ORIGINAL SPECIFIC GRAVITY (OG)	ALCOHOL by VOLUME
FINAL SPECIFIC GRAVITY (FG)	COLOR (SRMS)
APPARENT DEGREE of ACTUAL FERMENTATION	BITTERNESS (IBUS)

RECORDS

DATE	WEEKS after BOTTLING
TASTERS PRESENT	
COMMENTS	

First Tasting

DATE	WEEKS after BOTTLING
TASTERS PRESENT	
COMMENTS	

Second Tasting

AROMA	OVERALL IMPRESSION
COLOR/APPEARANCE	
FLAVOR	
MOUTHFEEL/BODY	

Tasting Notes

OVERALL RATING

☐ FLOP ☐ DRINKABLE ☐ MOST ENJOYABLE ☐ EXCEPTIONAL

Beer tasting usually involves evaluating the following five features in the order given: (1) aroma; (2) color and appearance; (3) flavor; (4) mouthfeel and body; (5) overall impression and aftertaste. (See Glossary for definitions.)

THE BEERMAKER'S RECORD BOOK

Who & Where

BEERMAKING SITE	CO-BEERMAKERS

The Details

RECIPE No.	% ALCOHOL
COMMERCIAL NAME	BOTTLE SIZE
BREWCASTLE NAME	$ per DOZ.
TYPE of BREW	$ per BATCH
DESCRIPTION	DATE MADE
	DATE BOTTLED
	No. of BOTTLES

Recipe Sheet

MALT (VOL. per)	
FERMENTABLES	
GRAIN (WT. per)	
HOPS (WT. per)	
YEAST (WT. or AMT.)	
ADDITIONAL NOTES	

Vital Stats

ORIGINAL SPECIFIC GRAVITY (OG)	ALCOHOL by VOLUME
FINAL SPECIFIC GRAVITY (FG)	COLOR (SRMS)
APPARENT DEGREE of ACTUAL FERMENTATION	BITTERNESS (IBUS)

RECORDS

DATE	WEEKS after BOTTLING
TASTERS PRESENT	
COMMENTS	

First Tasting

DATE	WEEKS after BOTTLING
TASTERS PRESENT	
COMMENTS	

Second Tasting

AROMA	OVERALL IMPRESSION
COLOR/APPEARANCE	
FLAVOR	
MOUTHFEEL/BODY	

Tasting Notes

OVERALL RATING

☐ FLOP ☐ DRINKABLE ☐ MOST ENJOYABLE ☐ EXCEPTIONAL

Beer tasting usually involves evaluating the following five features in the order given: (1) aroma; (2) color and appearance; (3) flavor; (4) mouthfeel and body; (5) overall impression and aftertaste. (See Glossary for definitions.)

THE BEERMAKER'S RECORD BOOK

Who & Where

BEERMAKING SITE	CO-BEERMAKERS

The Details

RECIPE No.	% ALCOHOL
COMMERCIAL NAME	BOTTLE SIZE
BREWCASTLE NAME	$ per DOZ.
TYPE of BREW	$ per BATCH
DESCRIPTION	DATE MADE
	DATE BOTTLED
	No. of BOTTLES

Recipe Sheet

MALT (VOL. per)	
FERMENTABLES	
GRAIN (WT. per)	
HOPS (WT. per)	
YEAST (WT. or AMT.)	
ADDITIONAL NOTES	

Vital Stats

ORIGINAL SPECIFIC GRAVITY (OG)	ALCOHOL by VOLUME
FINAL SPECIFIC GRAVITY (FG)	COLOR (SRMS)
APPARENT DEGREE of ACTUAL FERMENTATION	BITTERNESS (IBUS)

RECORDS

DATE	WEEKS after BOTTLING
TASTERS PRESENT	
COMMENTS	

First Tasting

DATE	WEEKS after BOTTLING
TASTERS PRESENT	
COMMENTS	

Second Tasting

AROMA	OVERALL IMPRESSION
COLOR/APPEARANCE	
FLAVOR	
MOUTHFEEL/BODY	

Tasting Notes

OVERALL RATING

☐ FLOP   ☐ DRINKABLE   ☐ MOST ENJOYABLE   ☐ EXCEPTIONAL

Beer tasting usually involves evaluating the following five features in the order given: (1) aroma; (2) color and appearance; (3) flavor; (4) mouthfeel and body; (5) overall impression and aftertaste. (See Glossary for definitions.)

THE BEERMAKER'S RECORD BOOK

Who & Where

BEERMAKING SITE	CO-BEERMAKERS

The Details

RECIPE No.	% ALCOHOL
COMMERCIAL NAME	BOTTLE SIZE
BREWCASTLE NAME	$ per DOZ.
TYPE of BREW	$ per BATCH
DESCRIPTION	DATE MADE
	DATE BOTTLED
	No. of BOTTLES

Recipe Sheet

MALT (vol. per)	
FERMENTABLES	
GRAIN (wt. per)	
HOPS (wt. per)		
YEAST (wt. or amt.)	
ADDITIONAL NOTES	

Vital Stats

ORIGINAL SPECIFIC GRAVITY (og)	ALCOHOL by VOLUME
FINAL SPECIFIC GRAVITY (fg)	COLOR (srms)
APPARENT DEGREE of ACTUAL FERMENTATION	BITTERNESS (ibus)

RECORDS

DATE	WEEKS after BOTTLING
TASTERS PRESENT	
COMMENTS	

First Tasting

DATE	WEEKS after BOTTLING
TASTERS PRESENT	
COMMENTS	

Second Tasting

AROMA	OVERALL IMPRESSION
COLOR/APPEARANCE	
FLAVOR	
MOUTHFEEL/BODY	

Tasting Notes

OVERALL RATING

☐ FLOP   ☐ DRINKABLE   ☐ MOST ENJOYABLE   ☐ EXCEPTIONAL

Beer tasting usually involves evaluating the following five features in the order given: (1) aroma; (2) color and appearance; (3) flavor; (4) mouthfeel and body; (5) overall impression and aftertaste. (See Glossary for definitions.)

THE BEERMAKER'S RECORD BOOK

Who & Where

BEERMAKING SITE	CO-BEERMAKERS

The Details

RECIPE No.	% ALCOHOL
COMMERCIAL NAME	BOTTLE SIZE
BREWCASTLE NAME	$ per DOZ.
TYPE of BREW	$ per BATCH
DESCRIPTION	DATE MADE
	DATE BOTTLED
	No. of BOTTLES

Recipe Sheet

MALT (VOL. per)	
FERMENTABLES	
GRAIN (WT. per)	
HOPS (WT. per)	
YEAST (WT. or AMT.)	
ADDITIONAL NOTES	

Vital Stats

ORIGINAL SPECIFIC GRAVITY (OG)	ALCOHOL by VOLUME
FINAL SPECIFIC GRAVITY (FG)	COLOR (SRMS)
APPARENT DEGREE of ACTUAL FERMENTATION	BITTERNESS (IBUS)

RECORDS

DATE		WEEKS after BOTTLING
TASTERS PRESENT		
COMMENTS		

First Tasting

DATE		WEEKS after BOTTLING
TASTERS PRESENT		
COMMENTS		

Second Tasting

AROMA	OVERALL IMPRESSION
COLOR/APPEARANCE	
FLAVOR	
MOUTHFEEL/BODY	

Tasting Notes

OVERALL RATING

☐ FLOP ☐ DRINKABLE ☐ MOST ENJOYABLE ☐ EXCEPTIONAL

Beer tasting usually involves evaluating the following five features in the order given: (1) aroma; (2) color and appearance; (3) flavor; (4) mouthfeel and body; (5) overall impression and aftertaste. (See Glossary for definitions.)

THE BEERMAKER'S RECORD BOOK

Who & Where

BEERMAKING SITE	CO-BEERMAKERS

The Details

RECIPE No.	% ALCOHOL
COMMERCIAL NAME	BOTTLE SIZE
BREWCASTLE NAME	$ per DOZ.
TYPE of BREW	$ per BATCH
DESCRIPTION	DATE MADE
	DATE BOTTLED
	No. of BOTTLES

Recipe Sheet

MALT (vol. per)	
FERMENTABLES	
GRAIN (wt. per)	
HOPS (wt. per)	
YEAST (wt. or amt.)	
ADDITIONAL NOTES	

Vital Stats

ORIGINAL SPECIFIC GRAVITY (og)	ALCOHOL by VOLUME
FINAL SPECIFIC GRAVITY (fg)	COLOR (srms)
APPARENT DEGREE of ACTUAL FERMENTATION	BITTERNESS (ibus)

RECORDS

DATE	WEEKS after BOTTLING
TASTERS PRESENT	
COMMENTS	

First Tasting

DATE	WEEKS after BOTTLING
TASTERS PRESENT	
COMMENTS	

Second Tasting

AROMA	OVERALL IMPRESSION
COLOR/APPEARANCE	
FLAVOR	
MOUTHFEEL/BODY	

Tasting Notes

OVERALL RATING

☐ FLOP   ☐ DRINKABLE   ☐ MOST ENJOYABLE   ☐ EXCEPTIONAL

Beer tasting usually involves evaluating the following five features in the order given: (1) aroma; (2) color and appearance; (3) flavor; (4) mouthfeel and body; (5) overall impression and aftertaste. (See Glossary for definitions.)

THE BEERMAKER'S RECORD BOOK

Who & Where

BEERMAKING SITE	CO-BEERMAKERS

The Details

RECIPE No.	% ALCOHOL
COMMERCIAL NAME	BOTTLE SIZE
BREWCASTLE NAME	$ per DOZ.
TYPE of BREW	$ per BATCH
DESCRIPTION	DATE MADE
	DATE BOTTLED
	No. of BOTTLES

Recipe Sheet

- MALT (VOL. per)
- FERMENTABLES
- GRAIN (WT. per)
- HOPS (WT. per)
- YEAST (WT. or AMT.)
- ADDITIONAL NOTES

Vital Stats

ORIGINAL SPECIFIC GRAVITY (OG)	ALCOHOL by VOLUME
FINAL SPECIFIC GRAVITY (FG)	COLOR (SRMS)
APPARENT DEGREE of ACTUAL FERMENTATION	BITTERNESS (IBUS)

RECORDS

DATE		WEEKS after BOTTLING
TASTERS PRESENT		
COMMENTS		

First Tasting

DATE		WEEKS after BOTTLING
TASTERS PRESENT		
COMMENTS		

Second Tasting

AROMA	OVERALL IMPRESSION
COLOR/APPEARANCE	
FLAVOR	
MOUTHFEEL/BODY	

Tasting Notes

OVERALL RATING

☐ FLOP   ☐ DRINKABLE   ☐ MOST ENJOYABLE   ☐ EXCEPTIONAL

Beer tasting usually involves evaluating the following five features in the order given: (1) aroma; (2) color and appearance; (3) flavor; (4) mouthfeel and body; (5) overall impression and aftertaste. (See Glossary for definitions.)

THE BEERMAKER'S RECORD BOOK

Who & Where

BEERMAKING SITE	CO-BEERMAKERS

The Details

RECIPE No.	% ALCOHOL
COMMERCIAL NAME	BOTTLE SIZE
BREWCASTLE NAME	$ per DOZ.
TYPE of BREW	$ per BATCH
DESCRIPTION	DATE MADE
	DATE BOTTLED
	No. of BOTTLES

Recipe Sheet

- MALT (VOL. per)
- FERMENTABLES
- GRAIN (WT. per)
- HOPS (WT. per)
- YEAST (WT. or AMT.)
- ADDITIONAL NOTES

Vital Stats

ORIGINAL SPECIFIC GRAVITY (OG)	ALCOHOL by VOLUME
FINAL SPECIFIC GRAVITY (FG)	COLOR (SRMS)
APPARENT DEGREE of ACTUAL FERMENTATION	BITTERNESS (IBUS)

RECORDS

DATE	WEEKS after BOTTLING
TASTERS PRESENT	
COMMENTS	

First Tasting

DATE	WEEKS after BOTTLING
TASTERS PRESENT	
COMMENTS	

Second Tasting

AROMA	OVERALL IMPRESSION
COLOR/APPEARANCE	
FLAVOR	
MOUTHFEEL/BODY	

Tasting Notes

OVERALL RATING

☐ FLOP   ☐ DRINKABLE   ☐ MOST ENJOYABLE   ☐ EXCEPTIONAL

Beer tasting usually involves evaluating the following five features in the order given: (1) aroma; (2) color and appearance; (3) flavor; (4) mouthfeel and body; (5) overall impression and aftertaste. (See Glossary for definitions.)

THE BEERMAKER'S RECORD BOOK

Who & Where

BEERMAKING SITE	CO-BEERMAKERS

The Details

RECIPE No.	% ALCOHOL
COMMERCIAL NAME	BOTTLE SIZE
BREWCASTLE NAME	$ per DOZ.
TYPE of BREW	$ per BATCH
DESCRIPTION	DATE MADE
	DATE BOTTLED
	No. of BOTTLES

Recipe Sheet

MALT (VOL. per)	
FERMENTABLES	
GRAIN (WT. per)	
HOPS (WT. per)	
YEAST (WT. or AMT.)	
ADDITIONAL NOTES	

Vital Stats

ORIGINAL SPECIFIC GRAVITY (OG)	ALCOHOL by VOLUME
FINAL SPECIFIC GRAVITY (FG)	COLOR (SRMS)
APPARENT DEGREE of ACTUAL FERMENTATION	BITTERNESS (IBUS)

RECORDS

DATE	WEEKS after BOTTLING
TASTERS PRESENT	
COMMENTS	

First Tasting

DATE	WEEKS after BOTTLING
TASTERS PRESENT	
COMMENTS	

Second Tasting

AROMA	OVERALL IMPRESSION
COLOR/APPEARANCE	
FLAVOR	
MOUTHFEEL/BODY	

Tasting Notes

OVERALL RATING

☐ FLOP ☐ DRINKABLE ☐ MOST ENJOYABLE ☐ EXCEPTIONAL

Beer tasting usually involves evaluating the following five features in the order given: (1) aroma; (2) color and appearance; (3) flavor; (4) mouthfeel and body; (5) overall impression and aftertaste. (See Glossary for definitions.)

THE BEERMAKER'S RECORD BOOK

Who & Where

BEERMAKING SITE	CO-BEERMAKERS

The Details

RECIPE No.	% ALCOHOL
COMMERCIAL NAME	BOTTLE SIZE
BREWCASTLE NAME	$ per DOZ.
TYPE of BREW	$ per BATCH
DESCRIPTION	DATE MADE
	DATE BOTTLED
	No. of BOTTLES

Recipe Sheet

MALT (vol. per)	
FERMENTABLES	
GRAIN (wt. per)	
HOPS (wt. per)		
YEAST (wt. or amt.)	
ADDITIONAL NOTES	

Vital Stats

ORIGINAL SPECIFIC GRAVITY (OG)	ALCOHOL by VOLUME
FINAL SPECIFIC GRAVITY (FG)	COLOR (SRMS)
APPARENT DEGREE of ACTUAL FERMENTATION	BITTERNESS (IBUS)

RECORDS

DATE	WEEKS after BOTTLING
TASTERS PRESENT	
COMMENTS	

First Tasting

DATE	WEEKS after BOTTLING
TASTERS PRESENT	
COMMENTS	

Second Tasting

AROMA	OVERALL IMPRESSION
COLOR/APPEARANCE	
FLAVOR	
MOUTHFEEL/BODY	

Tasting Notes

OVERALL RATING

☐ FLOP   ☐ DRINKABLE   ☐ MOST ENJOYABLE   ☐ EXCEPTIONAL

Beer tasting usually involves evaluating the following five features in the order given: (1) aroma; (2) color and appearance; (3) flavor; (4) mouthfeel and body; (5) overall impression and aftertaste. (See Glossary for definitions.)

THE BEERMAKER'S RECORD BOOK

Who & Where

BEERMAKING SITE	CO-BEERMAKERS

The Details

RECIPE No.	% ALCOHOL
COMMERCIAL NAME	BOTTLE SIZE
BREWCASTLE NAME	$ per DOZ.
TYPE of BREW	$ per BATCH
DESCRIPTION	DATE MADE
	DATE BOTTLED
	No. of BOTTLES

Recipe Sheet

MALT (VOL. per)	
FERMENTABLES	
GRAIN (WT. per)	
HOPS (WT. per)	
YEAST (WT. or AMT.)	
ADDITIONAL NOTES	

Vital Stats

ORIGINAL SPECIFIC GRAVITY (OG)	ALCOHOL by VOLUME
FINAL SPECIFIC GRAVITY (FG)	COLOR (SRMS)
APPARENT DEGREE of ACTUAL FERMENTATION	BITTERNESS (IBUS)

RECORDS

DATE	WEEKS after BOTTLING
TASTERS PRESENT	
COMMENTS	

First Tasting

DATE	WEEKS after BOTTLING
TASTERS PRESENT	
COMMENTS	

Second Tasting

AROMA	OVERALL IMPRESSION
COLOR/APPEARANCE	
FLAVOR	
MOUTHFEEL/BODY	

Tasting Notes

OVERALL RATING

☐ FLOP   ☐ DRINKABLE   ☐ MOST ENJOYABLE   ☐ EXCEPTIONAL

Beer tasting usually involves evaluating the following five features in the order given: (1) aroma; (2) color and appearance; (3) flavor; (4) mouthfeel and body; (5) overall impression and aftertaste. (See Glossary for definitions.)

THE BEERMAKER'S RECORD BOOK

Who & Where

BEERMAKING SITE	CO-BEERMAKERS

The Details

RECIPE No.	% ALCOHOL
COMMERCIAL NAME	BOTTLE SIZE
BREWCASTLE NAME	$ per DOZ.
TYPE of BREW	$ per BATCH
DESCRIPTION	DATE MADE
	DATE BOTTLED
	No. of BOTTLES

Recipe Sheet

MALT (VOL. per)	
FERMENTABLES	
GRAIN (WT. per)	
HOPS (WT. per)	
YEAST (WT. or AMT.)	
ADDITIONAL NOTES	

Vital Stats

ORIGINAL SPECIFIC GRAVITY (OG)	ALCOHOL by VOLUME
FINAL SPECIFIC GRAVITY (FG)	COLOR (SRMS)
APPARENT DEGREE of ACTUAL FERMENTATION	BITTERNESS (IBUS)

RECORDS

DATE	WEEKS after BOTTLING
TASTERS PRESENT	
COMMENTS	

First Tasting

DATE	WEEKS after BOTTLING
TASTERS PRESENT	
COMMENTS	

Second Tasting

AROMA	OVERALL IMPRESSION
COLOR/APPEARANCE	
FLAVOR	
MOUTHFEEL/BODY	

Tasting Notes

OVERALL RATING

☐ FLOP   ☐ DRINKABLE   ☐ MOST ENJOYABLE   ☐ EXCEPTIONAL

Beer tasting usually involves evaluating the following five features in the order given: (1) aroma; (2) color and appearance; (3) flavor; (4) mouthfeel and body; (5) overall impression and aftertaste. (See Glossary for definitions.)

THE BEERMAKER'S RECORD BOOK

Who & Where

BEERMAKING SITE	CO-BEERMAKERS

The Details

RECIPE No.	% ALCOHOL
COMMERCIAL NAME	BOTTLE SIZE
BREWCASTLE NAME	$ per DOZ.
TYPE of BREW	$ per BATCH
DESCRIPTION	DATE MADE
	DATE BOTTLED
	No. of BOTTLES

Recipe Sheet

MALT (VOL. per)	
FERMENTABLES	
GRAIN (WT. per)	
HOPS (WT. per)	
YEAST (WT. or AMT.)	
ADDITIONAL NOTES	

Vital Stats

ORIGINAL SPECIFIC GRAVITY (OG)	ALCOHOL by VOLUME
FINAL SPECIFIC GRAVITY (FG)	COLOR (SRMS)
APPARENT DEGREE of ACTUAL FERMENTATION	BITTERNESS (IBUS)

RECORDS

DATE		WEEKS after BOTTLING
TASTERS PRESENT		
COMMENTS		

First Tasting

DATE		WEEKS after BOTTLING
TASTERS PRESENT		
COMMENTS		

Second Tasting

AROMA	OVERALL IMPRESSION
COLOR/APPEARANCE	
FLAVOR	
MOUTHFEEL/BODY	

Tasting Notes

OVERALL RATING

☐ FLOP   ☐ DRINKABLE   ☐ MOST ENJOYABLE   ☐ EXCEPTIONAL

Beer tasting usually involves evaluating the following five features in the order given: (1) aroma; (2) color and appearance; (3) flavor; (4) mouthfeel and body; (5) overall impression and aftertaste. (See Glossary for definitions.)

THE BEERMAKER'S RECORD BOOK

Who & Where

BEERMAKING SITE	CO-BEERMAKERS

The Details

RECIPE No.	% ALCOHOL
COMMERCIAL NAME	BOTTLE SIZE
BREWCASTLE NAME	$ per DOZ.
TYPE of BREW	$ per BATCH
DESCRIPTION	DATE MADE
	DATE BOTTLED
	No. of BOTTLES

Recipe Sheet

MALT (VOL. per)		
FERMENTABLES		
GRAIN (WT. per)		
HOPS (WT. per)		
YEAST (WT. or AMT.)		
ADDITIONAL NOTES		

Vital Stats

ORIGINAL SPECIFIC GRAVITY (OG)	ALCOHOL by VOLUME
FINAL SPECIFIC GRAVITY (FG)	COLOR (SRMS)
APPARENT DEGREE of ACTUAL FERMENTATION	BITTERNESS (IBUS)

RECORDS

DATE	WEEKS after BOTTLING
TASTERS PRESENT	
COMMENTS	

First Tasting

DATE	WEEKS after BOTTLING
TASTERS PRESENT	
COMMENTS	

Second Tasting

AROMA	OVERALL IMPRESSION
COLOR/APPEARANCE	
FLAVOR	
MOUTHFEEL/BODY	

Tasting Notes

OVERALL RATING

☐ FLOP   ☐ DRINKABLE   ☐ MOST ENJOYABLE   ☐ EXCEPTIONAL

Beer tasting usually involves evaluating the following five features in the order given: (1) aroma; (2) color and appearance; (3) flavor; (4) mouthfeel and body; (5) overall impression and aftertaste. (See Glossary for definitions.)

THE BEERMAKER'S RECORD BOOK

Who & Where

BEERMAKING SITE	CO-BEERMAKERS

The Details

RECIPE No.	% ALCOHOL
COMMERCIAL NAME	BOTTLE SIZE
BREWCASTLE NAME	$ per DOZ.
TYPE of BREW	$ per BATCH
DESCRIPTION	DATE MADE
	DATE BOTTLED
	No. of BOTTLES

Recipe Sheet

MALT (VOL. per)	
FERMENTABLES	
GRAIN (WT. per)	
HOPS (WT. per)		
YEAST (WT. or AMT.)	
ADDITIONAL NOTES	

Vital Stats

ORIGINAL SPECIFIC GRAVITY (OG)	ALCOHOL by VOLUME
FINAL SPECIFIC GRAVITY (FG)	COLOR (SRMS)
APPARENT DEGREE of ACTUAL FERMENTATION	BITTERNESS (IBUS)

RECORDS

DATE	WEEKS after BOTTLING
TASTERS PRESENT	
COMMENTS	

First Tasting

DATE	WEEKS after BOTTLING
TASTERS PRESENT	
COMMENTS	

Second Tasting

AROMA	OVERALL IMPRESSION
COLOR/APPEARANCE	
FLAVOR	
MOUTHFEEL/BODY	

Tasting Notes

OVERALL RATING

☐ FLOP ☐ DRINKABLE ☐ MOST ENJOYABLE ☐ EXCEPTIONAL

Beer tasting usually involves evaluating the following five features in the order given: (1) aroma; (2) color and appearance; (3) flavor; (4) mouthfeel and body; (5) overall impression and aftertaste. (See Glossary for definitions.)

THE BEERMAKER'S RECORD BOOK

Who & Where

BEERMAKING SITE	CO-BEERMAKERS

The Details

RECIPE No.	% ALCOHOL
COMMERCIAL NAME	BOTTLE SIZE
BREWCASTLE NAME	$ per DOZ.
TYPE of BREW	$ per BATCH
DESCRIPTION	DATE MADE
	DATE BOTTLED
	No. of BOTTLES

Recipe Sheet

MALT (vol. per)	
FERMENTABLES	
GRAIN (wt. per)	
HOPS (wt. per)		
YEAST (wt. or amt.)	
ADDITIONAL NOTES	

Vital Stats

ORIGINAL SPECIFIC GRAVITY (og)	ALCOHOL by VOLUME
FINAL SPECIFIC GRAVITY (fg)	COLOR (srms)
APPARENT DEGREE of ACTUAL FERMENTATION	BITTERNESS (ibus)

RECORDS

DATE	WEEKS after BOTTLING
TASTERS PRESENT	
COMMENTS	

First Tasting

DATE	WEEKS after BOTTLING
TASTERS PRESENT	
COMMENTS	

Second Tasting

AROMA	OVERALL IMPRESSION
COLOR/APPEARANCE	
FLAVOR	
MOUTHFEEL/BODY	

Tasting Notes

OVERALL RATING

☐ FLOP   ☐ DRINKABLE   ☐ MOST ENJOYABLE   ☐ EXCEPTIONAL

Beer tasting usually involves evaluating the following five features in the order given: (1) aroma; (2) color and appearance; (3) flavor; (4) mouthfeel and body; (5) overall impression and aftertaste. (See Glossary for definitions.)

THE BEERMAKER'S RECORD BOOK

Who & Where

BEERMAKING SITE	CO-BEERMAKERS

The Details

RECIPE No.	% ALCOHOL
COMMERCIAL NAME	BOTTLE SIZE
BREWCASTLE NAME	$ per DOZ.
TYPE of BREW	$ per BATCH
DESCRIPTION	DATE MADE
	DATE BOTTLED
	No. of BOTTLES

Recipe Sheet

MALT (VOL. per)	
FERMENTABLES	
GRAIN (WT. per)	
HOPS (WT. per)		
YEAST (WT. or AMT.)	
ADDITIONAL NOTES	

Vital Stats

ORIGINAL SPECIFIC GRAVITY (OG)	ALCOHOL by VOLUME
FINAL SPECIFIC GRAVITY (FG)	COLOR (SRMS)
APPARENT DEGREE of ACTUAL FERMENTATION	BITTERNESS (IBUS)

RECORDS

DATE	WEEKS after BOTTLING
TASTERS PRESENT	
COMMENTS	

First Tasting

DATE	WEEKS after BOTTLING
TASTERS PRESENT	
COMMENTS	

Second Tasting

AROMA	OVERALL IMPRESSION
COLOR/APPEARANCE	
FLAVOR	
MOUTHFEEL/BODY	

Tasting Notes

OVERALL RATING

☐ FLOP   ☐ DRINKABLE   ☐ MOST ENJOYABLE   ☐ EXCEPTIONAL

Beer tasting usually involves evaluating the following five features in the order given: (1) aroma; (2) color and appearance; (3) flavor; (4) mouthfeel and body; (5) overall impression and aftertaste. (See Glossary for definitions.)

THE BEERMAKER'S RECORD BOOK

Who & Where

BEERMAKING SITE	CO-BEERMAKERS

The Details

RECIPE No.	% ALCOHOL
COMMERCIAL NAME	BOTTLE SIZE
BREWCASTLE NAME	$ per DOZ.
TYPE of BREW	$ per BATCH
DESCRIPTION	DATE MADE
	DATE BOTTLED
	No. of BOTTLES

Recipe Sheet

- MALT (VOL. per)
- FERMENTABLES
- GRAIN (WT. per)
- HOPS (WT. per)
- YEAST (WT. or AMT.)
- ADDITIONAL NOTES

Vital Stats

ORIGINAL SPECIFIC GRAVITY (OG)	ALCOHOL by VOLUME
FINAL SPECIFIC GRAVITY (FG)	COLOR (SRMS)
APPARENT DEGREE of ACTUAL FERMENTATION	BITTERNESS (IBUS)

RECORDS

DATE	WEEKS after BOTTLING
TASTERS PRESENT	
COMMENTS	

First Tasting

DATE	WEEKS after BOTTLING
TASTERS PRESENT	
COMMENTS	

Second Tasting

AROMA	OVERALL IMPRESSION
COLOR/APPEARANCE	
FLAVOR	
MOUTHFEEL/BODY	

Tasting Notes

OVERALL RATING

☐ FLOP ☐ DRINKABLE ☐ MOST ENJOYABLE ☐ EXCEPTIONAL

Beer tasting usually involves evaluating the following five features in the order given: (1) aroma; (2) color and appearance; (3) flavor; (4) mouthfeel and body; (5) overall impression and aftertaste. (See Glossary for definitions.)

THE BEERMAKER'S RECORD BOOK

Who & Where

BEERMAKING SITE	CO-BEERMAKERS

The Details

RECIPE No.	% ALCOHOL
COMMERCIAL NAME	BOTTLE SIZE
BREWCASTLE NAME	$ per DOZ.
TYPE of BREW	$ per BATCH
DESCRIPTION	DATE MADE
	DATE BOTTLED
	No. of BOTTLES

Recipe Sheet

MALT (VOL. per)	
FERMENTABLES	
GRAIN (WT. per)	
HOPS (WT. per)		
YEAST (WT. or AMT.)	
ADDITIONAL NOTES	

Vital Stats

ORIGINAL SPECIFIC GRAVITY (OG)	ALCOHOL by VOLUME
FINAL SPECIFIC GRAVITY (FG)	COLOR (SRMS)
APPARENT DEGREE of ACTUAL FERMENTATION	BITTERNESS (IBUS)

RECORDS

DATE	WEEKS after BOTTLING
TASTERS PRESENT	
COMMENTS	

First Tasting

DATE	WEEKS after BOTTLING
TASTERS PRESENT	
COMMENTS	

Second Tasting

AROMA	OVERALL IMPRESSION
COLOR/APPEARANCE	
FLAVOR	
MOUTHFEEL/BODY	

Tasting Notes

OVERALL RATING

☐ FLOP   ☐ DRINKABLE   ☐ MOST ENJOYABLE   ☐ EXCEPTIONAL

Beer tasting usually involves evaluating the following five features in the order given: (1) aroma; (2) color and appearance; (3) flavor; (4) mouthfeel and body; (5) overall impression and aftertaste. (See Glossary for definitions.)

THE BEERMAKER'S RECORD BOOK

Who & Where

BEERMAKING SITE	CO-BEERMAKERS

The Details

RECIPE No.	% ALCOHOL
COMMERCIAL NAME	BOTTLE SIZE
BREWCASTLE NAME	$ per DOZ.
TYPE of BREW	$ per BATCH
DESCRIPTION	DATE MADE
	DATE BOTTLED
	No. of BOTTLES

Recipe Sheet

MALT (VOL. per)	
FERMENTABLES	
GRAIN (WT. per)	
HOPS (WT. per)	
YEAST (WT. or AMT.)	
ADDITIONAL NOTES	

Vital Stats

ORIGINAL SPECIFIC GRAVITY (OG)	ALCOHOL by VOLUME
FINAL SPECIFIC GRAVITY (FG)	COLOR (SRMS)
APPARENT DEGREE of ACTUAL FERMENTATION	BITTERNESS (IBUS)

RECORDS

DATE	WEEKS after BOTTLING
TASTERS PRESENT	
COMMENTS	

First Tasting

DATE	WEEKS after BOTTLING
TASTERS PRESENT	
COMMENTS	

Second Tasting

AROMA	OVERALL IMPRESSION
COLOR/APPEARANCE	
FLAVOR	
MOUTHFEEL/BODY	

Tasting Notes

OVERALL RATING

☐ FLOP ☐ DRINKABLE ☐ MOST ENJOYABLE ☐ EXCEPTIONAL

Beer tasting usually involves evaluating the following five features in the order given: (1) aroma; (2) color and appearance; (3) flavor; (4) mouthfeel and body; (5) overall impression and aftertaste. (See Glossary for definitions.)

THE BEERMAKER'S RECORD BOOK

Who & Where

BEERMAKING SITE	CO-BEERMAKERS

The Details

RECIPE No.	% ALCOHOL
COMMERCIAL NAME	BOTTLE SIZE
BREWCASTLE NAME	$ per DOZ.
TYPE of BREW	$ per BATCH
DESCRIPTION	DATE MADE
	DATE BOTTLED
	No. of BOTTLES

Recipe Sheet

MALT (VOL. per)	
FERMENTABLES	
GRAIN (WT. per)	
HOPS (WT. per)			
YEAST (WT. or AMT.)	
ADDITIONAL NOTES	

Vital Stats

ORIGINAL SPECIFIC GRAVITY (OG)	ALCOHOL by VOLUME
FINAL SPECIFIC GRAVITY (FG)	COLOR (SRMS)
APPARENT DEGREE of ACTUAL FERMENTATION	BITTERNESS (IBUS)

RECORDS

DATE	WEEKS after BOTTLING
TASTERS PRESENT	
COMMENTS	

First Tasting

DATE	WEEKS after BOTTLING
TASTERS PRESENT	
COMMENTS	

Second Tasting

AROMA	OVERALL IMPRESSION
COLOR/APPEARANCE	
FLAVOR	
MOUTHFEEL/BODY	

Tasting Notes

OVERALL RATING

☐ FLOP ☐ DRINKABLE ☐ MOST ENJOYABLE ☐ EXCEPTIONAL

Beer tasting usually involves evaluating the following five features in the order given: (1) aroma; (2) color and appearance; (3) flavor; (4) mouthfeel and body; (5) overall impression and aftertaste. (See Glossary for definitions.)

THE BEERMAKER'S RECORD BOOK

Who & Where

BEERMAKING SITE	CO-BEERMAKERS

The Details

RECIPE No.	% ALCOHOL
COMMERCIAL NAME	BOTTLE SIZE
BREWCASTLE NAME	$ per DOZ.
TYPE of BREW	$ per BATCH
DESCRIPTION	DATE MADE
	DATE BOTTLED
	No. of BOTTLES

Recipe Sheet

MALT (vol. per)	
FERMENTABLES	
GRAIN (wt. per)	
HOPS (wt. per)	
YEAST (wt. or amt.)	
ADDITIONAL NOTES	

Vital Stats

ORIGINAL SPECIFIC GRAVITY (og)	ALCOHOL by VOLUME
FINAL SPECIFIC GRAVITY (fg)	COLOR (srms)
APPARENT DEGREE of ACTUAL FERMENTATION	BITTERNESS (ibus)

RECORDS

DATE		WEEKS after BOTTLING
TASTERS PRESENT		
COMMENTS		

First Tasting

DATE		WEEKS after BOTTLING
TASTERS PRESENT		
COMMENTS		

Second Tasting

AROMA	OVERALL IMPRESSION
COLOR/APPEARANCE	
FLAVOR	
MOUTHFEEL/BODY	

Tasting Notes

OVERALL RATING

☐ FLOP   ☐ DRINKABLE   ☐ MOST ENJOYABLE   ☐ EXCEPTIONAL

Beer tasting usually involves evaluating the following five features in the order given: (1) aroma; (2) color and appearance; (3) flavor; (4) mouthfeel and body; (5) overall impression and aftertaste. (See Glossary for definitions.)

THE BEERMAKER'S RECORD BOOK

Who & Where

BEERMAKING SITE	CO-BEERMAKERS

The Details

RECIPE No.	% ALCOHOL
COMMERCIAL NAME	BOTTLE SIZE
BREWCASTLE NAME	$ per DOZ.
TYPE of BREW	$ per BATCH
DESCRIPTION	DATE MADE
	DATE BOTTLED
	No. of BOTTLES

Recipe Sheet

MALT (VOL. per)		
FERMENTABLES		
GRAIN (WT. per)		
HOPS (WT. per)		
YEAST (WT. or AMT.)		
ADDITIONAL NOTES		

Vital Stats

ORIGINAL SPECIFIC GRAVITY (OG)	ALCOHOL by VOLUME
FINAL SPECIFIC GRAVITY (FG)	COLOR (SRMS)
APPARENT DEGREE of ACTUAL FERMENTATION	BITTERNESS (IBUS)

RECORDS

DATE	WEEKS after BOTTLING
TASTERS PRESENT	
COMMENTS	

First Tasting

DATE	WEEKS after BOTTLING
TASTERS PRESENT	
COMMENTS	

Second Tasting

AROMA	OVERALL IMPRESSION
COLOR/APPEARANCE	
FLAVOR	
MOUTHFEEL/BODY	

Tasting Notes

OVERALL RATING

☐ FLOP ☐ DRINKABLE ☐ MOST ENJOYABLE ☐ EXCEPTIONAL

Beer tasting usually involves evaluating the following five features in the order given: (1) aroma; (2) color and appearance; (3) flavor; (4) mouthfeel and body; (5) overall impression and aftertaste. (See Glossary for definitions.)

THE BEERMAKER'S RECORD BOOK

Who & Where

BEERMAKING SITE	CO-BEERMAKERS

The Details

RECIPE No.	% ALCOHOL
COMMERCIAL NAME	BOTTLE SIZE
BREWCASTLE NAME	$ per DOZ.
TYPE of BREW	$ per BATCH
DESCRIPTION	DATE MADE
	DATE BOTTLED
	No. of BOTTLES

Recipe Sheet

MALT (VOL. per)	
FERMENTABLES	
GRAIN (WT. per)	
HOPS (WT. per)		
YEAST (WT. or AMT.)	
ADDITIONAL NOTES	

Vital Stats

ORIGINAL SPECIFIC GRAVITY (OG)	ALCOHOL by VOLUME
FINAL SPECIFIC GRAVITY (FG)	COLOR (SRMS)
APPARENT DEGREE of ACTUAL FERMENTATION	BITTERNESS (IBUS)

RECORDS

DATE	WEEKS after BOTTLING
TASTERS PRESENT	
COMMENTS	

First Tasting

DATE	WEEKS after BOTTLING
TASTERS PRESENT	
COMMENTS	

Second Tasting

AROMA	OVERALL IMPRESSION
COLOR/APPEARANCE	
FLAVOR	
MOUTHFEEL/BODY	

Tasting Notes

OVERALL RATING

☐ FLOP ☐ DRINKABLE ☐ MOST ENJOYABLE ☐ EXCEPTIONAL

Beer tasting usually involves evaluating the following five features in the order given: (1) aroma; (2) color and appearance; (3) flavor; (4) mouthfeel and body; (5) overall impression and aftertaste. (See Glossary for definitions.)

THE BEERMAKER'S RECORD BOOK

Who & Where

BEERMAKING SITE	CO-BEERMAKERS

The Details

RECIPE No.	% ALCOHOL
COMMERCIAL NAME	BOTTLE SIZE
BREWCASTLE NAME	$ per DOZ.
TYPE of BREW	$ per BATCH
DESCRIPTION	DATE MADE
	DATE BOTTLED
	No. of BOTTLES

Recipe Sheet

MALT (VOL. per)	
FERMENTABLES	
GRAIN (WT. per)	
HOPS (WT. per)		
YEAST (WT. or AMT.)	
ADDITIONAL NOTES	

Vital Stats

ORIGINAL SPECIFIC GRAVITY (OG)	ALCOHOL by VOLUME
FINAL SPECIFIC GRAVITY (FG)	COLOR (SRMS)
APPARENT DEGREE of ACTUAL FERMENTATION	BITTERNESS (IBUS)

RECORDS

DATE	WEEKS after BOTTLING
TASTERS PRESENT	
COMMENTS	

First Tasting

DATE	WEEKS after BOTTLING
TASTERS PRESENT	
COMMENTS	

Second Tasting

AROMA	OVERALL IMPRESSION
COLOR/APPEARANCE	
FLAVOR	
MOUTHFEEL/BODY	

Tasting Notes

OVERALL RATING

☐ FLOP   ☐ DRINKABLE   ☐ MOST ENJOYABLE   ☐ EXCEPTIONAL

Beer tasting usually involves evaluating the following five features in the order given: (1) aroma; (2) color and appearance; (3) flavor; (4) mouthfeel and body; (5) overall impression and aftertaste. (See Glossary for definitions.)

THE BEERMAKER'S RECORD BOOK

Who & Where

BEERMAKING SITE	CO-BEERMAKERS

The Details

RECIPE No.	% ALCOHOL
COMMERCIAL NAME	BOTTLE SIZE
BREWCASTLE NAME	$ per DOZ.
TYPE of BREW	$ per BATCH
DESCRIPTION	DATE MADE
	DATE BOTTLED
	No. of BOTTLES

Recipe Sheet

MALT (VOL. per)	
FERMENTABLES	
GRAIN (WT. per)	
HOPS (WT. per)	
YEAST (WT. or AMT.)	
ADDITIONAL NOTES	

Vital Stats

ORIGINAL SPECIFIC GRAVITY (OG)	ALCOHOL by VOLUME
FINAL SPECIFIC GRAVITY (FG)	COLOR (SRMs)
APPARENT DEGREE of ACTUAL FERMENTATION	BITTERNESS (IBUS)

RECORDS

DATE	WEEKS after BOTTLING
TASTERS PRESENT	
COMMENTS	

First Tasting

DATE	WEEKS after BOTTLING
TASTERS PRESENT	
COMMENTS	

Second Tasting

AROMA	OVERALL IMPRESSION
COLOR/APPEARANCE	
FLAVOR	
MOUTHFEEL/BODY	

Tasting Notes

OVERALL RATING

☐ FLOP   ☐ DRINKABLE   ☐ MOST ENJOYABLE   ☐ EXCEPTIONAL

Beer tasting usually involves evaluating the following five features in the order given: (1) aroma; (2) color and appearance; (3) flavor; (4) mouthfeel and body; (5) overall impression and aftertaste. (See Glossary for definitions.)

ADDITIONAL COMMENTS AND LABELS

ADDITIONAL COMMENTS AND LABELS

ADDITIONAL COMMENTS AND LABELS

ADDITIONAL COMMENTS AND LABELS

THE BEERMAKER'S RECORD BOOK

NAME	
ADDRESS	
PHONE	FAX

NAME	
ADDRESS	
PHONE	FAX

NAME	
ADDRESS	
PHONE	FAX

NAME	
ADDRESS	
PHONE	FAX

NAME	
ADDRESS	
PHONE	FAX

ADDRESSES AND CONTACT NUMBERS

NAME	
ADDRESS	
PHONE	FAX

NAME	
ADDRESS	
PHONE	FAX

NAME	
ADDRESS	
PHONE	FAX

NAME	
ADDRESS	
PHONE	FAX

NAME	
ADDRESS	
PHONE	FAX

THE BEERMAKER'S RECORD BOOK

NAME
ADDRESS
PHONE	FAX

NAME
ADDRESS
PHONE	FAX

NAME
ADDRESS
PHONE	FAX

NAME
ADDRESS
PHONE	FAX

NAME
ADDRESS
PHONE	FAX

ADDRESSES AND CONTACT NUMBERS

NAME

ADDRESS

PHONE	FAX

NAME

ADDRESS

PHONE	FAX

NAME

ADDRESS

PHONE	FAX

NAME

ADDRESS

PHONE	FAX

NAME

ADDRESS

PHONE	FAX

BEER-TASTING TERMS

What care I how time advances?
I am drinking ale today.
– Edgar Allan Poe

ALE: One of the two main types of beer (the other being lager). Ale is fermented at a warmer temperature (with more ingredients) than lager, resulting in a robust beer with a fruitier yeast and a complex taste and aroma.

AROMA: The distinctive, usually pleasant scent of a beer. A beer's most prominent aromas come from its malt and hops content (see definitions for HOPPY and MALTY below).

BITTER: A beer with a pronounced hop character; leaves a dry, astringent taste on the back of your tongue.

BODY: The perceived fullness of a beer in your mouth. The body of a beer can range from watery to light and from medium to heavy (a full-bodied brew).

COLOR RANGE: A beer's color is generally classified as pale, golden, amber, brown, or black.

COMPLEXITY: A feature that is important to a beer's satisfaction rating. A brew's complexity refers to the variety of flavors and sensations on your palate as you taste the beer.

CRISP: A highly carbonated, bubbly, and refreshing beer.

ESTERY: An unpredictable by-product of the fermentation process that results in a beer with fruity aromas.

FINISH: The aftertaste left by a beer; rounds out your overall impression of the product.

FLAVOR INTENSITY: The intensity of a beer's flavor ranges from lacking, faint, and mild to moderate, strong, and intense. A balanced beer is one in which the flavors of the malt, hops, and fermentables are harmonious.

HOPPY: When the flavor of the hops is prominent in a beer, thus imparting a herbal and spicy aroma and bitter taste. The opposite of a malty beer.

LAGER: One of the two main types of beer (the other being ale). Lager is fermented at a cooler temperature (with fewer ingredients) than ale, resulting in a beer that is light and crisp with a fresh, balanced taste and aroma.

MALTY: The sweet, caramelly, roasty, or chocolaty aroma of a beer. The opposite of a hoppy beer.

MOUTHFEEL: The physical texture and sensation – alcoholic warmth, carbonation, dryness, etc. – of a beer in your mouth and throat. The mouthfeel of a beer can range from light and thin to full-bodied and thick.

ROBUST: A bold, full-bodied beer.

We hope you enjoyed using *The Beermaker's Record Book*.

We welcome your comments and suggestions, and will incorporate the best ideas into future editions. We will also send a complimentary copy of the next edition to anyone who sends in a suggestion that we are able to use. Address your comments to:

Project Editor
The Beermaker's Record Book
Raincoast Books
8680 Cambie Street
Vancouver, B.C.
Canada v6p 6m9